Dedication

This guidebook is dedicated to every person who bravely attempts new things, hungrily seeks to learn new tools, and who actively comes to the table desiring to make new friends. I welcome you to the social mix and am so excited that you are about to join the social conversation. This book is dedicated to you.

About the author:

Kathryn Rose

Kathryn is a social media strategist, trainer, author and speaker whose clients include major brands, international organizations, small businesses, and entrepreneurs.

In her twenty-year sales and marketing career, Kathryn has become a specialist in increasing sales through collaborative strategies. As a Vice President of Sales at the Wall Street firm, Credit Suisse, she built a referral network that helped her increase sales to over $100m per year. She also created Connecticut's first cable television cooperative marketing alliance, as well as the Arts Marketing cooperative, which helped clients with limited marketing budgets achieve economies of scale.

She is a sought after speaker and trainer on using social media for maximum online visibility and using online marketing and social media tools to create referral networks and to increase sales. As an author, her books include: The Step by Step Guide to Facebook for

Business, The Step by Step Guide to Twitter for Business, The Step by Guide to SEO/Video Marketing for Business and The Step by Step Guide to Linkedin for Business and The Parent's and Grandparent's Guides to Facebook.

Her speaking events include the Ladies Who Launch Global Conference, Real Estate University and Loan Officer Magazine. She has also spoken to school districts in Canada and the U.S. about online safety for children.

Connect with Kathryn on

Website: http://katroseconsulting.com

Facebook : http://facebook.com/katrose

Twitter: http://twitter.com/katkrose

Linkedin: http://linkedin.com/in/katkrose

Updated: March 2011

Table of Contents

Chapter 1 - Facebook for Business: The Relevance

There has been so much buzz about using Facebook for business in the past few years that you are probably wondering about the how and why of it all. Up until now, you may have been associating Facebook with teenagers, friends, family and fun. While Facebook did start as a membership site for Harvard college students, it has since expanded to a global powerhouse and is currently ranked as one of the most used social networking sites worldwide. Today, Facebook has more than 500 million registered global users, and is ranked as the second most visited site on the internet.

If you are wondering how this information can be relevant to your business, the answer is simple: Your target market lives here.

Consider these Facebook Statistics (statistics sourced from Facebook unless otherwise noted):

➢ **Facebook has over 500+ million users.**

- If Facebook were a country, it would be the 3rd largest in the world.
- Over 9 million U.S. children between the ages of 13 and 17 are registered Facebook users. (source http://www.checkfacebook.com.)
- 50% of active users log on to Facebook in any given day.
- The average Facebook user has 130 friends.
- People spend over 500 billion minutes per month on Facebook.

Activity on Facebook
- There are over 160 million interaction points for users (pages, groups and events).
- The average user is connected to 60 pages, groups and events.
- The average user creates 70 pieces of content each month.

- ➢ **More than 25 billion bits of content (web links, news stories, blog posts, notes, photo albums, etc.) are shared each month.**

Global Reach

- ➢ **More than 70 language translations are available on the site.**
- ➢ **About 70% of Facebook users are outside the United States.**

The two fastest growing demographics on Facebook are people aged 35 or older and those who are over 55. My 86 year-old uncle sent me a friend request the other day!

What does all this really mean? Facebook users are a mature audience, most of which have a college degree, have the time to network, and possess the money to spend.

With Facebook Fan Pages, also called Business Pages, Facebook has not only become a place for people to connect and network, but it has also become another avenue for businesses and organizations to connect and network with customers, partners and vendors.

Facebook business pages are public and therefore indexed by Google. This is the most important benefit and is the point of leverage for your presence on Facebook. This is why Facebook pages stand out as an excellent investment of time when it comes to creating a visibility strategy for your business. If I haven't convinced you yet, let us just mention that more than 10 million Facebook users become fans of individual pages each day. People actively choose to 'like' such brands as Coke, Starbucks, Zappos, Target, and Walmart. They do so because they want a relationship with a particular brand. They believe that by becoming a part of a brand's community on Facebook, they'll receive special offers, discounts, and advance notice of new offerings.

When your business has a fan page on Facebook, you have the opportunity to have the same interactions with potential customers and clients that Fortune 500 companies do. Facebook offers every business the same level playing field as a pathway to reach an extremely large audience. Doesn't it make good business sense to be a part of that?

Can you have a business presence on Facebook without creating a fan page? The answer is 'yes' and 'no.' It is against Facebook's terms of use to have a personal profile with a business name. But you can use your personal profile for business. Confused? Let me clear it up for you. You must sign up for a personal profile with your REAL NAME. You cannot have a personal profile with the name 'ABC Company' or Kathryn ABC Company. Facebook will allow you to register it, but if someone reports your misuse of the personal profile platform or Facebook does a random check (and this happens), they will shut your profile down and you will lose all the friends and posts you've created.

A Facebook business page, however, must be used with a business name. If you decide you do not have time to manage both a personal and a business page, you can, through my 'Strategic Friending Formula,' connect with people in your target market for business using your personal profile.

In other words, you can talk about business related things on your personal profile, but in order to have a page devoted to your business, with your business name attached, you'll want to have a Facebook business page (also referred to as a 'fan' page because prior to 'likes' people became 'fans' of a page). Another reason to have a Fan Page is that Facebook only allows you to have up to 5000 'friends,' while Business Pages can have unlimited followers. So if you're working to create a very large following, a Fan (or business) Page is the way to go.

Creating a Facebook page for your business is the most effective way of marketing on Facebook, especially if your marketing budget is tight. I will show you how to create your Facebook Fan Page, engage in conversation and create a community of raving fans.

Before I take you on the journey of creating your own Fan Page and making a presence on Facebook for your business, I will start by having you create your own personal profile and become familiar and comfortable with the site.

Although you can create a page for your business even if you do not have a personal profile, there are advantages to creating a personal profile first. By having your own personal profile, Facebook allows you to create richer content for your page. As a registered user, you will be allowed to use many more applications that have been developed just for the enhancement of Fan Pages. A much more limited selection is available to you if you do not have a profile.

With the updates in 2011, Facebook has made it more beneficial than ever to have a business page on the platform. Businesses can now comment and 'like' other pages, unlike in prior versions. As we go through the book, I will point out some of the new features to make your experience on Facebook as profitable as possible.

Chapter 2- Create Your Facebook Profile

If you don't already have a Facebook profile, please take the time to read this chapter and set one up. All you need to set up a Facebook profile is a legitimate email address. Facebook will send you an email to confirm your user information, and you will then have to verify it from that e-mail address. This is a step that Facebook requires to insure the validity and security of your newly created account.

If you already have a profile, I suggest you check your privacy settings and be familiar with how to edit the important information that may affect the way you represent yourself and your business. Be professional and make sure you represent your business in the same way you would represent yourself to potential clients in person. Small details are sometimes left out, and I want to make sure you are aware of easy fixes that may make a world of difference in the online presentation of yourself and your business.

Here's how to set up a profile:

Go to http://Facebook .com

Enter your information and create an account.

"Facebook was created to make the world more open and transparent, which in turn will create greater understanding and connection. Facebook promotes openness and transparency by giving individuals greater power to share and connect," as they state in their Terms documents. "People should have the freedom to build trust and reputation through their identity and *connections, and should not have their presence on the Facebook Service removed for reasons other than those described in Facebook's Statement of Rights and Responsibilities."* Please make sure you are familiar with these documents, and follow and respect the principles described in order to have the best experience.

Step 1: Find Friends

I do not recommend you give up your email list—ever, but if you would like to start connecting quickly with friends, then go ahead and enter your email address and password when prompted. This will allow Facebook to temporarily access your e-mail account and cross check your contacts with Facebook's database. If this makes you uncomfortable or nervous, just click 'skip this step.'

Step 2: Profile Info

On this page, you will be asked about your school information. You do not have to fill this out either.

Facebook tries to narrow down your profile so it can suggest friends for you. It is up to you if you want to enter this information. If you do not want to give this information now, you can always add it later, so click 'skip.'

Step 3: Profile Picture

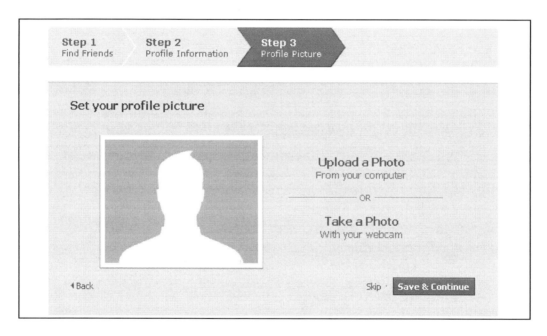

You should have your picture uploaded as soon as possible. People like to see the faces of the people they are interacting with and are more likely to engage more often with profiles possessing a photo. When choosing your picture, please take into consideration that you will be communicating with other professionals and potential clients. Because you are here to make an impression, to engage with others, and to network for the benefit of your business, it is important that the picture you upload represents you as a professional.

The process of uploading a photo is very easy. Click on 'upload a photo.' Then find the photo on your computer and click 'upload.' If you have a webcam, you can take a photo directly from your computer and use that as well. When you are satisfied with the photo, press 'save & continue.' You can, and should, change your photo over time, in order to match any significant changes in your appearance (such as to hair length and color). Clients and business contacts who meet you for the first time but have only known you through Facebook should be able to say: "I recognize you from your Facebook photo." Don't use a picture from 20 years ago, your kid's picture, that one of you on vacation in Hawaii, show YOU.

Once you finish Step 3, you will come to this screen:

f Welcome to Facebook,

1 Search your email for friends already on Facebook

Your Email: [I]

Find Friends

2 Upload a profile picture

Upload a Photo
From your computer

------- OR -------

Take a Photo
With your webcam

3 Fill out your profile information

Help your friends find you by filling out some basic profile information.

✎ Edit Profile

4 Activate your mobile phone

- Receive texts with your friends' Status Updates and Messages instantly.
- Update your Status and Message friends using SMS.

Register for Facebook Text Messages

Already received a confirmation code?

5 Find people you know

Search by name or look for classmates and coworkers.

[Enter a name or email] [🔍]

6 Control what information you share

Learn more about privacy on Facebook.

If you have already uploaded a picture, step 2 will not be visible.

Let's move to step 3: Fill out your Profile information.

Chapter 3 - Fill out Your Profile Information

After you create your profile, it's time to populate your information.

If you just finished setting up a profile, click on 'Edit Profile' here:

If you already have a profile, you will find the 'Edit Profile' area under your name on the 'home page.'

Entering your information in these fields is completely voluntary. You do not need to answer *any* of the questions in this section or fill out any information. You may include some, all or none of the information that Facebook asks you to provide here.

Here are the areas of information that you can fill in:

- ➤ **Basic Information**
- ➤ **Profile Picture**
- ➤ **Featured People**
- ➤ **Education and Work Information**
- ➤ **Philosophy**
- ➤ **Arts and Entertainment**
- ➤ **Sports**
- ➤ **Activities and Interests**
- ➤ **Contact Information**

As you start populating these sections, keep in mind how you want to be represented online as a professional. Share the information that will help you gain leverage, position you as an expert and help you attract a community you can engage with happily and productively.

Basic Information: This section collects your basic information, and it is not necessary for you to answer all the questions.

It is recommended that you NEVER show your full birthday in your profile. This is the kind of information that can lead to identity theft. Facebook's default setting is: 'Show my full birthday in my profile.' To change this, click on the drop down arrow and change it to: 'Show only month and day.' If you don't want your birthday to show up at all, change it to: 'Don't show my birthday in my profile.' Facebook is a social network, however, and wishing people a happy birthday is a widespread practice; so, you may want to consider showing at least your month and day.

Current City and Hometown may very well be relevant if you are trying to connect to local people or to help people who may want to be able to find you.

However, the 'Interested In' may be something you want to keep private. Again, none of these fields is required. Fill them in according to your comfort level.

I would recommend that you fill in the 'About Me' section with your bio.

Profile picture: Previously I talked about the importance of uploading a profile photo. Well, you can upload several photos, in fact. You can rotate the photos on your profile. Also, Facebook will show, in a mini-photo album of sorts, the last 5 photos that you uploaded. I will get into photo sharing a little later.

Featured people:

Relationship Status:	Married ⌄ to

Family:		Select Relation: ⌄ ✕

Add another family member

Featured Friends: Create new list

Save Changes

In this area, you can enter information such as your relationship status, your partner's name (with a link to your partner's profile), your children's and other family members' again, linking to their profiles. Remember, none of this information is required; it is completely at your discretion. I do not recommend you add young family member's names to your profile - especially those of young children.

There is another area called 'Featured Friends.' Here, you can select specific groups of friends to be shown at all times on your Facebook profile. To create a featured list, either go to the featured people area or go to the friends area on your profile and click on the "pencil" icon, which will bring you to the featured people screen.

Education and Work: The next screen to view and update is the Education & Work screen. Here's where you'll have the opportunity to add your High School, College and University details. Facebook also uses this information to suggest potential connections with other graduates from the same schools. This is a great way to connect socially and professionally with people from your past. If you feel comfortable sharing your work information, go ahead and enter it as well.

Philosophy: On this screen you can choose to fill in your religious beliefs, political views, etc. I recommend that, unless your religious beliefs or political views are related to your business objectives, they be left blank.

Arts and Entertainment, Sports and Activities and Interests: These sections allow you to fill out music, books, television shows, sports teams and topics you like. This information can be used for Facebook to suggest friends to you, and Facebook uses it to target advertising.

You may want to fill this out because it can be a great tool to keep an eye on your competition. For example, if you fill out the interests area and put 'social media' as one of your activities or interests, Facebook will provide targeted content to you via advertising. All Facebook ads relating to anything social media will be displayed. This way you can see what your competition is up to or obtain some good information, such as what the competition offers to other people; free reports; teleseminars, or perhaps special discounts.

Remember, all of this information will be available to your friends, to friends of your friends or to whomever you decide to share your profile with (based on your privacy settings, which I will cover in great detail in the next chapters). So let's say that your business targets Yankee baseball fans but you are really a Red Sox fan and so list the latter team as one of your 'likes.' That might not be something you want to do.

Contact information: Consider this area to be your extended business card, a place where you can creatively and succinctly tell friends, family and potential new clients exactly what you do and how to reach you in order to ask you about your products or services.

Choose wisely when filling out this section. Do you want everyone to have your cell phone number? How important is it to post your address? Your website should be listed in this format: http://yourwebsiteurl.com. Including the 'http://' makes the link clickable.

Now that you are done editing your profile, let's move on to Account Settings.

Chapter 4 - Account Settings

In this chapter I'll review your Account Settings. This covers the overall configuration of your account, name, and user ID, as well as some additional things such as notifications and language. You can access the Account Settings from the drop down menu on the top blue navigation bar, all the way to the right, under 'Account.'

- On the **Settings tab**, check to be sure all of your information is correct.

- Under 'Name,' if you have a maiden name or another name you go by, you may want to add it here.

- Username: Facebook allows you to create a unique username for your profile; this makes it easy to share with friends or to put on your business card. A personal url will look like this http://facebook.com/katrose (which is my username).

- Email: you can see what your contact email looks like. You will also have the option to adjust your privacy settings regarding contact information. I will cover privacy in detail later in this book.

- Password: change or update your password here.

- Linked accounts: you can link your account to your email accounts and other outside accounts, but I suggest that you keep your Facebook account separate from other networks to keep tighter security levels on your passwords.

- Security Question: if you ever have to contact Facebook, this will be the question they ask to identify you as the account owner.

- Privacy: You can access the privacy screens from here. However, as mentioned, I will be covering privacy in detail in the next few chapters.

- Account Security: This is an important area. This area was made more robust after Mark Zuckerberg's (yes, the founder of Facebook) account was hacked.

These settings allow you to set a secure browsing option (which I highly recommend) and be notified if someone tries to access your account from a computer or mobile device that you have not used before. This way if someone is trying to "hijack" or "hack" your account, you will be notified.

In this screen shot, the person entering their information only has email set up at this time. You can set up a mobile phone with Facebook and this feature will also ask if you want to be notified via text message. If you have a text-enabled phone I recommend that you set it up so you can be instantly notified.

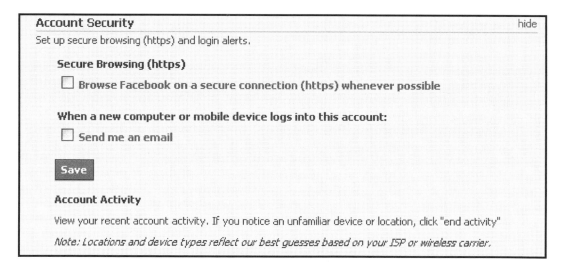

What if you get a notification that someone has hacked your account? Immediately change your password.

- Download Your Information: Facebook added this option so you can download your photos and other information if you wish.

- Deactivate Account – this is self explanatory.

We will now move to the second tab: **The Networks Tab**.

My Account

Settings	Networks	Notifications	Mobile	Language	Payments

Facebook is made up of many networks, each based around a workplace, region, high school, or college. Join a network to discover the people who work, live or study around you.

You aren't in any networks.

Enter a city, workplace, school or region. →

Join a Network

Enter a workplace or school.

Network name:

[Join Network]

This will allow you to join a network of friends, colleagues, or classmates if you would like. Joining different networks may help you establish a broader presence and find more relevant contacts. For example, if you have a local business, it would make sense to enter a city and connect with local people who may refer business to you.

The Notifications Tab: This feature allows you to turn on and off notifications for events, notices, and other actions your friends take that are relevant to you. I find it beneficial to be notified right away with *some* of the actions, but annoying for other actions. Take time to explore your options and choose what is appropriate for you. You can always come back and adjust your settings as you become more familiar with how you use Facebook.

You can send your notifications to your cell phone via SMS, but before you do this, it would be wise to be sure that your wireless plan supports a text message option.

Mobile Tab: This is a place where you can activate your smart phone (Blackberry, iPhone, or similar), so that you will be able to post your status updates, or upload photos and videos, from your phone. You can also set-up your account to receive text message notifications for updates for different actions. Note that standard text messaging fees may apply, depending on your mobile service plan.

Language Tab: Facebook is now available in more than 70 languages. You can choose your language preference from the drop down menu.

Payments: You can make some purchases via Facebook, but most people set this up for purchasing Facebook advertising for their business. I recommend that you set this up only when and if you would like to purchase Facebook Social Ads to promote your business.

Facebook Ads Tab: Although Facebook says they will not use your photos in ads, I recommend that you configure this setting "no one." Facebook could possibly use your personal information for Facebook social ads in the future.

Also, Facebook lets your friends know when you've 'liked' an advertisement on Facebook. You may not want this information to be shared with all of your friends. To opt out, scroll down to the bottom and select 'no one' in the permissions field as well.

Chapter 5 – Privacy Settings

The question I get the most when I am out speaking to organizations and entrepreneurs about Facebook is: "How can I keep my personal life private but use my personal account for business?"

Here is my simple answer: Don't try. Sure Facebook has a detailed privacy platform, which I have outlined in this chapter; but I have made the decision to use my Facebook personal profile as a business marketing tool. I do at times post status updates that talk about my son and some bits about my personal life but nothing that I wouldn't say at a Chamber of Commerce networking function. That is one of the differences in using Facebook for business. Think of it as a large networking party. Would you talk about personal things about your family or show those pictures of your kids in the bathtub out at a networking function? If the answer is "no," then don't post it on Facebook.

Again, you can configure your privacy settings so that your personal information can be hidden; but if you are 'friending' 5000 people (the Facebook friend limit) to network for business, why take the chance that something personal may pop up?

That being said, I want to arm you with the privacy information so that you have a good understanding of what can and may be accessible to others on Facebook, and so that you can make choices about how to set them to your comfort level.

To access the 'Privacy Settings' screen, go over to the upper right hand corner of your Facebook profile on the blue navigation bar and click on the 'Account' tab; then choose 'Privacy Settings.'

Choose Your Privacy Settings

Connecting on Facebook
Control basic information your friends will use to find you on Facebook. View Settings

Sharing on Facebook
These settings control who can see what you share.

	Everyone	Friends of Friends	Friends Only
Your status, photos, and posts	•		
Bio and favorite quotations	•		
Family and relationships	•		
Photos and videos you're tagged in		•	
Religious and political views		•	
Birthday		•	
Permission to comment on your posts			•
Places you check in to [?]			•
Contact information			•

Everyone

Friends of Friends

Friends Only

Recommended ✔

☑ Share a tagged post with friends of the friend I tag

✏ Customize settings   ✔ This is your current setting.

Apps and Websites
Edit your settings for using apps, games and websites.

Block Lists
Edit your lists of blocked people and apps.

Controlling How You Share
Learn more about your privacy on Facebook.

As you can see, Facebook has a "recommended" default privacy setting configuration. Unfortunately, in some cases those settings are the *least* private. Here is a detailed explanation of the main three privacy settings.

1. **Everyone – This is not just everyone on Facebook. This is everyone on the INTERNET.** This information is indexed

by Google's search engine as well other search engines.

2. **Friends of Friends – This means all of the people you 'friended' AND <u>all</u> of <u>their</u> friends.** Many people do not understand what this means; so I always take the time to explain it clearly. Let's say you have not 'friended' your boss, but you have 'friended' a co-worker who HAS 'friended' your boss. If you have your settings configured to 'friends of friends,' your boss will be able to see that area of Facebook. If your 'wall' settings are set to 'friends of friends' and you make a post about how much you hate your boss, he or she will be able to see it. Now might be a good time to remind you that what you post on Facebook should always be considered to be public, no matter what your privacy settings are set to. Use common sense and don't post things you wouldn't want others to see.

3. **Only Friends – This means that only people you 'friend' can see your profile information.** But remember:

if you're using Facebook and 'friending' for business, this setting becomes less private.

You also have the option to 'Customize Settings.'

Choose Your Privacy Settings			
Connecting on Facebook Control basic information your friends will use to find you on Facebook . View Settings			
Sharing on Facebook These settings control who can see what you share.			
	Everyone	Friends of Friends	Friends Only
Everyone	Your status, photos, and posts	•	
Friends of Friends	Bio and favorite quotations	•	
Friends Only	Family and relationships	•	
	Photos and videos you're tagged in		•
	Religious and political views		•
Recommended ✓	Birthday		•
	Permission to comment on your posts		•
	Places you check in to [?]		•
	Contact information		•
	☑ Share a tagged post with friends of the friend I tag		
	✎ Customize settings	✓ This is your current setting.	
Apps and Websites Edit your settings for using apps, games and websites.	**Block Lists** Edit your lists of blocked people and apps.	**Controlling How You Share** Learn more about your privacy on Facebook .	

If you click 'Customize,' you will be taken to this screen, which has these and other privacy choices:

Choose Your Privacy Settings▸ Customize settings

◂ Back to Privacy   Preview My Profile

Customize who can see and comment on things you share, things on your Wall and things you're tagged in.

Things I share

Posts by me Default setting for posts, including status updates and photos	🔒 Everyone ▾
Family	🔒 Everyone ▾
Relationships	🔒 Everyone ▾
Interested in and looking for	🔒 Everyone ▾
Bio and favorite quotations	🔒 Everyone ▾
Website	🔒 Everyone ▾
Religious and political views	🔒 Friends of Friends ▾
Birthday	🔒 Friends of Friends ▾

Edit album privacy for existing photos.

If you click on the drop down box next to each of the choices, you can further customize your exposure:

Choose Your Privacy Settings▸ Customize settings

◂ Back to Privacy   Preview My Profile

Customize who can see and comment on things you share, things on your Wall and things you're tagged in.

Things I share

Posts by me
Default setting for posts, including status updates and photos

🔒 Everyone ▾

• **Everyone**
Friends of Friends
Friends Only
Customize

Family

Relationships

Once you click on 'Customize' on this screen, you will see that the phrase 'Hide this from' is a choice. Here, you can manually select friends that you would like to exclude.

Custom Privacy

✓ **Make this visible to**

These people: Only Friends   ▼

Friends of Friends
Only Friends
Specific People...
Only Me

✗ **Hide this from**

These people: Enter a Name or List

Save Setting   Cancel

Using the 'Posts by me' setting as an example, customizing this setting may be useful if you post often about your business and if this information is not interesting to your family members. But if you find you are regularly hiding posts from the same people because you don't want them to know what you are doing, then you may want to consider simply 'unfriending' them. They won't be notified when you drop them from your friend list. The only way they can confirm that you have removed them as a friend is if they view your profile and the option to 'Add as Friend' is available. In other words, if they can now attempt to 'friend' you, they are no longer a 'friend.'

Towards the bottom of this screen there is an option 'Friends can post on my wall.' Make sure that this is 'enabled' to allow your friends to post on your wall and connect with you. If it's not checked, they will not be able to leave you messages, and your page will be a stagnant page, containing only your posts.

In addition, you can check how your profile looks to other people—**and I highly recommend doing so**—by clicking on the 'Preview My Profile' link in the upper right hand corner of the screen (see below).

This will show you how *most people* (Facebook's words) will see your profile when they visit you. You'll be able to double check how you've set your profile and correct any oversights.

Remember, you can always come back to this same spot, make changes, and adjust.

In many cases, I suggest that you don't even fill out any of this information. Categories like "interested in, looking for, family, religion or relationships" are areas that you may not necessarily want to share in a business relationship.

A couple of areas I want to draw your attention to are:

Bio or favorite quotation:

This is where you can tell people about you, your business or your blog, and share your website information. This information can be updated or changed whenever you choose. When using Facebook for business, I recommend this setting be configured to 'Everyone' so that it is public when people search for your profile on the Facebook platform, and so that it is indexed by Google and other search engines.

Edit Photo Album Privacy:

If you decide to upload photos, it is a good idea to set privacy levels for your photos on Facebook. In fact, you can set a different privacy level on each one of your photo albums. This is a great feature because you will be able to share your 'family' albums with your family, 'friend' albums with your Facebook friends, and thus keep personal albums private from the view of your business Facebook friends, if you wish.

Relationships:

As you can see in the example below, if you do not make your relationship status private, when you change your status, it posts to your and your friends newsfeeds. This may not be something you want to share with the world. As an example, to test this setting for this book, I changed

Susan Miller

Wall   Info   Photos   +

What's on your mind?

Attach: ▼   🔒▼   Share

View Photos of Me (1)   🔍 Options

Edit My Profile

RECENT ACTIVITY

♥ Susan went from being "single" to "in a relationship." · Comment · Like

my relationship status from 'married' to 'single.' The phone immediately started to ring. One of the phone calls was from my husband who wanted to know: "Is there something you wanted to talk about?" Oops.

I recommend that you don't even say that you are in a relationship in the first place; but if you do, you set it to ensure that no one is notified of any changes you make.

To make these notifications private, scroll down and set the 'Relationship' area to 'Only Me' by clicking on 'Customize' and selecting "Only Me' in a pop up window. This means that only you will be able to see your relationship status update change.

Customize who can see

Things I share

Custom Privacy

✓ **Make this visible to**

These people: | Only Me ▾ |

Only I can see this.

✗ **Hide this from**

These people: | Enter a Name or List |

Save Setting   Cancel

Only ▾

Only ▾

n ▾

Only ▾

e ▾

Photos and Videos I'm tagged in:

Things others share

Photos and videos I'm tagged in   🔒 Only Me ▾

Can comment on posts   🔒 Friends Only ▾
Includes status updates, friends' Wall posts, and photos

Friends can post on my Wall   ☑ Enable

Can see Wall posts by friends   🔒 Friends Only ▾

I personally don't want old pictures of me posted on Facebook for the world to see; so you may also think this privacy setting is quite important. For example, you can make sure that if people post photos of you and 'Tag' you in them, the photo will not automatically appear in your news stream or profile for all of your friends to see.

'Tagging' is a way for your friends to identify you in a post or photo, AND to notify you that they've posted something that may be of interest to you – such as pictures of you. When a photo is tagged, it appears in your news stream and profile for all of your friends to see, *unless* you've set your privacy settings to avoid this.

This setting is even more important now with the changes to Facebook's profile platform that occurred in late 2010. The last 5 photos that you either upload yourself or that your friends upload and TAG you in, will – by default – be visible on your profile.

Now you can't stop friends and relatives from posting unflattering, silly or embarrassing photos of you if they insist on doing so despite your protests. BUT if the photo does get posted and you wish it hadn't, you can certainly "Untag" yourself, so that at least the photo is not identified with your name and doesn't show up on your Facebook profile. To do this, click on the picture you've been 'Tagged' in and, beside your name under the photo, click on 'Remove tag.' This picture will no longer be linked to your profile on Facebook.

Here's an example of a photo tag gone wrong:

If you were Michael, you might not want your current business colleagues or future employers to see this photo. (provided by the blog http://myparentsjoinedfacebook.com).

Get those photo privacy settings in place!

To change this setting, much like the 'Relationship' area, go to 'Photos and videos I'm tagged in.' Then click 'Customize' and make sure it is set to 'Only Me.' This way, if a photo is uploaded and tagged, the only person who sees it is you, the profile owner.

Facebook Places

In August 2010, Facebook introduced 'Facebook Places' as a way to share where you are in real time by 'Checking In' via an application on your smart phone, like an iPhone or a blackberry. As of this writing, this feature is only available on the iphone, but it won't be long before it is available for blackberry and android.

Basically, 'Places' uses the GPS in your smart phone to let friends know what you're doing and where you are. The premise is if one of your friends sees you are at a particular place, they can come by and meet up with you.

If you do not choose to check in, your location is not reported. In other words, it won't tell people where you are, unless YOU share it.

This can be a dangerous thing: letting people know you are away from home. You cannot disable 'Places' per se, but you can choose not to use it. I recommend that you go in here and set the privacy for 'Places I check in to' to

"Only Me."

Places I check in to	🔒 Friends Only ▾
Include me in "People Here Now" after I check in Visible to friends and people checked in nearby (See an example)	☑ Enable

There are two other 'Places' settings to be aware of:

- **Include me in 'People Here Now' after I check in**: If you or your child 'checks in' to a place, Facebook will find other friends that are in the same place and let their friends know.

- **Friends can check me into places**: This setting allows friends to check you in. Imagine you called in sick to work and are really at the ball game. Your 'friend' innocently checks you in, when your boss and other co-workers are your Facebook friends. Not a good thing. Click on 'Friends can check me into places' and then click on 'Select One' and click 'Disable.'

Places: Friend Tags

Friends can check me in to Places   Select One ▼

You're in control of your location on Facebook:

- Facebook will never share or expose your location automatically
- Only friends can tag you and check you in to a place
- We'll notify you when a friend has tagged you
- As with photos, you can remove a friend's tag at any time

Learn more   **Okay**

Can see Wall posts by friends   🔒 Friends of Friends ▼

Friends can check me in to Places   Edit Settings 👆

Even though Facebook says you can remove the tag if you want to, the damage may already be done. Safest bet: disable the feature.

The rest of the choices are self-explanatory and I recommend you explore these on your own until you're familiar with them.

Chapter 6 - Contact Information

On the 'Facebook Customize' privacy screen, if you scroll to the bottom, you will find the 'contact information area.'

This area allows you to set restrictions about who can see your contact information, such as phone number, address, IM (Instant Message) Screen name (if applicable), and email address. Please remember my account of what it means to share this information with 'Everyone,' with 'Friends of Friends' and with 'Only

Friends.' Make your choice according to your comfort level. Again, you can change these at any time.

I do not recommend you make <u>any</u> *personal* information available to be viewed by 'Everyone.' However, because you are using Facebook for your business, you may choose to show your business phone number and address.

One area I want to draw your attention to here is your email address. This is the email address you used to sign up for Facebook. You may want to add an email address that is for business and to make only that one public.

Chapter 7 - Connecting on Facebook

Choose Your Privacy Settings

▣ **Connecting on Facebook**
Control basic information your friends will use to find you on Facebook. View Settings

---

This area controls how you share additional information, such as your hometown, how people can find you on Facebook, and what you 'like' on and off Facebook.

facebook 🔍 Search 🔍   Home Profile

Choose Your Privacy Settings▸   Basic Directory Information

◂ Back to Privacy		Preview My Profile

Your name, profile picture, gender and networks are always open to everyone (learn why). We suggest leaving the other basic settings below open to everyone to make it easier for real world friends to find and connect with you.

🔍 **Search for me on Facebook**	This lets friends find you on Facebook. If you're visible to fewer people, it may prevent you from connecting with your real world friends.	🔒 Everyone ▾
👥 **Send me friend requests**	This lets real world friends send you friend requests. If not set to everyone, it could prevent you from connecting with your friends.	🔒 Everyone ▾
💬 **Send me messages**	This lets friends you haven't connected with yet send you a message before adding you as a friend.	🔒 Everyone ▾
👥 **See my friend list**	This helps real world friends identify you by friends you have in common. Your friend list is always available to applications and your connections to friends may be visible elsewhere.	🔒 Only Me ▾
💼 **See my education and work**	This helps classmates and coworkers find you.	🔒 Everyone ▾
🏙 **See my current city and hometown**	This helps friends you grew up with and friends near you confirm it's really you.	🔒 Everyone ▾
✏ **See my interests and other Pages**	This lets you connect with people with common interests based on things you like on and off Facebook.	🔒 Friends Only ▾

Most of these settings are already defaulted to 'Everyone.' I suggest keeping them set that way to allow folks to find, 'friend' you and send you messages.

🔍 **Search for me on Facebook**	This lets friends find you on Facebook. If you're visible to fewer people, it may prevent you from connecting with your real world friends.	🔒 Everyone ▼ • Everyone Friends of Friends Friends Only
👥 **Send me friend**	This lets real world friends send you friend requests. If not set to	🔒 Everyone
👥 **Send me friend requests**	This lets real world friends send you friend requests. If not set to everyone, it could prevent you from connecting with your friends.	🔒 Everyone ▼
💬 **Send me messages**	This lets friends you haven't connected with yet send you a message before adding you as a friend.	🔒 Everyone ▼

Friends:

👥 **See my friend list**	This helps real world friends identify you by friends you have in common. Your friend list is always available to applications and your connections to friends may be visible elsewhere.	🔒 Only Me ▼

Facebook defaults to showing your friends list to 'Everyone.' It is up to you if you would like this list to be shown.

To change who can view your friends list, click on the drop down menu to the right of "See My Friend List" and choose your own level of comfort, keeping in mind what it means to share with 'Everyone.

The other areas are pretty self-explanatory, but the last thing I want to draw your attention to is the "See my interests and other Pages."

This was added after Facebook created the ability to add 'like' buttons across the web. For instance, you could be on a news website and 'like' an article. If you are logged in to your Facebook account, that information will be broadcast through your 'Newsfeed.' This may or may not be something you want to restrict.

See my interests and other Pages	This lets you connect with people with common interests based on things you like on and off Facebook.	🔒 Friends Only ▼
		Everyone
		Friends of Friends
		● **Friends Only**
		Customize

English (US)   About Advertising Develop

Chapter 8 - Privacy Settings - Apps and Websites

In the Applications and Websites area under Privacy Settings, you can control what information is accessible to any applications you use, as they may publish stories in your Notifications and News Feed sections. As you make your profile settings more restrictive, less information is available to these applications.

This area also houses your 'public search setting,' which dictates how people find your profile in a Google search or other search engine.

Once you click on 'Apps and Websites,' you will come to this screen:

If you have been on Facebook previously, you may have a list of applications that you have used or have allowed access in the past. To remove them from your profile, click 'Remove unwanted or spammy applications.' Or you can 'turn off all platform applications.'

To set restrictions on who can see your recent activity on games and applications, click on 'game and application activity.' Here you can configure your settings as you like.

In the area that says 'info accessible through your friends,' you will want to go through this and check the information that you want to allow your friends to share through the use of various applications on Facebook (like Birthday Calendar, or Greeting Card). Click on 'edit settings' and you will come to a screen that allows you to control information that is shared.

Info accessible through your friends

Use the settings below to control which of your information is available to applications, games and websites when your friends use them. The more info you share, the more social the experience.

- ☑ Bio
- ☑ Birthday
- ☐ Family and relationships
- ☐ Interested in and looking for
- ☐ Religious and political views
- ☑ My website
- ☐ If I'm online

- ☐ My status updates
- ☐ My photos
- ☐ My videos
- ☐ My links
- ☐ My notes
- ☐ Photos and videos I'm tagged in

Note: your name, profile picture, gender, networks and user ID (along with any other information you've set to everyone) is available to friends' applications unless you turn off platform applications and websites.

Save Changes   Cancel

The number of applications that is available can be overwhelming to say the least. Exercise caution every time you accept one. They often require permission from you to get all of your information as well as access to your friends' information, and, while you are having fun, the application is using that permission to track a variety of things about you and access your information!

These applications are free because using them gives the application owner permission to gather information about you and your friends that make up offline profiles, which are used as marketing data for some companies. Un-clicking your personal information will still give your friends access to the application, which will then simply no longer have access to your information.

I suggest you un-check all these items to keep your information yours. If you have any of your information set to 'Everyone,' you will see this reflected on this screen.

Some applications are fun, allowing you to do such things as send figurative flowers and gifts, and others can be royal time wasters (for me, these are things like mob wars, medieval knights, and little green patches). You'll decide through experience which ones you enjoy, and you can always delete any applications that you decide you do not like.

Some applications allow you to add information about yourself to your 'Wall' and some will allow you to do special things. An application called 'Events' will let you send an invitation for a specific activity to selected friends, and you might use this to set up a networking meeting, a party or to notify friends and fans about a personal appearance or workshop you are leading.

All of the games on Facebook are applications, and if you find that you and your friends enjoy these, they are a nice way to interact with people. However, they can be annoying to others; so use them (and invite others to join in) at your own risk. If you find that you don't enjoy having people post news or requests for farm animals or Mafia connections on your page, you can block those applications so that friends can no longer send you requests to play those particular games. And you can remove any applications you've downloaded if you decide later not to use them.

A very popular Facebook application is the Birthday Calendar application. This alerts you when any of the people on your friends list has a birthday coming up. You can then go to their page and wish them happy birthday. The application will automatically ask you if you want to give a birthday gift, but you don't need to do that. Just click the 'x' in the upper right hand corner of that box, get rid of the gifts option and write your happy birthday note in the space provided. This is a nice way to remember friends and colleagues on their special day and is one of the most used applications on Facebook.

The 'Instant Personalization' setting

In April, 2010, Facebook introduced an 'Open Graph' application, which they call 'Instant Personalization.' In my understanding, this is going to work much like amazon.com, where once I log in to Amazon it shows me titles and products I may be interested in, based upon past purchases. The idea is that users will want a personalized web experience; so, only content that matches their past likes will come up first.

What does this mean for you? Well, if you would like a more personalized experience, then this will be great for you. The downside is that this is an application, which can collect personal information about you via the application. Also, if your friends authorize the application, it may collect information that way as well. As of this writing, only three sites (Yelp.com, Pandora.com, and Docs.com) have permission to do such 'instant personalization' in a beta test.

How do you turn off the personalization? You can go to the 'instant personalization' setting and turn it off by un-checking the 'Allow" button. In my experience, this does not block the application from collecting information about you. You must go to the actual page and turn it off or say 'No thanks'. These three sites come up with a bar on the top saying: "Hi Kathryn, Docs is using Facebook to personalize your experience. Learn More – No Thanks."

You can, however, decide what personal information is shared by applications (by going, as I mentioned earlier, to the 'Info accessible through your friends' area and un-checking any information you do not want shared).

You can also prevent information from being shared by going back to all of the privacy settings and make sure that none of your settings is set to 'Everyone.' Facebook says:

What you share when visiting applications and websites

Applications you use will access your Facebook information in order for them to work. For example, a review application uses your location in order to surface restaurant recommendations.

*When you visit a Facebook-enhanced application or website, **it may access any information you have made*** *visible to Everyone, as well as your publicly available information. This includes your Name, Profile Picture, Gender, Current City, Networks, Friend List, and Pages. The application will request your permission to access any additional information it needs.*

What is the bottom line? Make sure your privacy settings are configured properly and do not share any information that you may not want accessed by applications. It is not necessary to divulge all of your personal information on Facebook.

Public Search Listing:

The last area I will focus on here is the 'Public search' area.

Public search	Show a preview of your Facebook profile when people look for you using a search engine.	**Edit Settings**

This setting controls whether or not your Facebook profile comes up in a search engine listing like Google. I recommend that you keep this 'Enabled' so that your potential clients and business associates can find your profile when doing an internet search.

You can see what your profile will look like in an internet search by clicking the 'see preview' button; again, it is suggested that you make sure to check out how your profile appears to the entire user base of the World Wide Web.

Facebook gets a huge amount of traffic from Google and other search engines. Not all of your profile is displayed; only the information you allowed to be publicly

shared when you set your privacy settings to 'Everyone.'
**Note: Potential employers and clients have been known to do a 'Google' search on prospective business associates. Things posted on the internet live forever. In light of this, these settings are extremely important.

Chapter 9 - Finding Friends

Now that you have your profile set up and the privacy settings configured to your comfort level, it's time to find friends.

There are several ways to find friends. The easiest way is to click on 'Find Friends' in the upper right of your blue navigation bar. If you have been on Facebook for a while and have a good number of friends, this option will not be shown. You can find friends either from the 'people you may know' area on the right of the page, or the 'Find Friends' area on the left:

Upon clicking here, you will be able to find friends via email address or by clicking 'show more' and then 'other tools' you can search for friends from past employers, classmates, etc.

Chapter 10 - Strategic Friending

When I advise clients to use their Facebook personal profile for business, I speak to them about a concept known as 'Strategic Friending.' The principle is really very simple. Identify your target audience, find them on Facebook and then send them friend requests.

For example, with my Realtor® clients, I recommend friending "anyone they have ever known who may want to buy a house from them now or in the future." Small business consultants will want to find and friend small business owners.

Finding friends is very easy on Facebook. The easiest way to start is by finding people you know. Simply type their name into the search bar and click the looking glass symbol.

Once you have entered your search query, review your results (see example below). As you can see on the very

Left side of the page, you can narrow your search by People, Pages, Groups, etc. This is highly valuable in cases where Facebook produces massive search results on several pages.

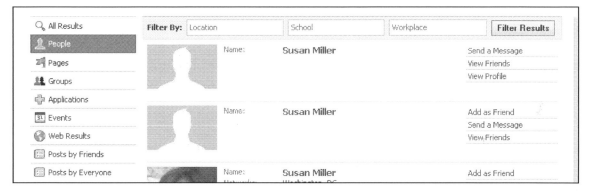

The same people you communicate with on a regular basis by email, or instant messaging, may be also be found on Facebook and become your friends. This is how you can search for them:

Facebook gives you the opportunity of employing several options for finding your friends and connecting with them. Explore them on your own and see how many different ways there are to find and connect with people on Facebook.

Another way of getting to that same screen is through your 'Account' link, located in the main top bar menu. Click on 'Edit Friends.'

Facebook will also offer to help you find new friends by suggesting people who have mutual interests or mutual friends. Look on the main dashboard 'Home' page on the right upper corner, underneath the 'Requests' section. There is an area there called 'Suggestions.' Facebook will make suggestions for you based on your account information settings, your recent activity, the pages you follow, and on your friends. To add a new friend from the suggestion list, you will need to click on the 'Add as Friend' link and then send a request for friendship. It is always a best practice to create a personal message to accompany your request, just to let your new future friend know why you are contacting them and how they may benefit from becoming your friend.

If your business is not so personal, you may consider strategically friending influencers and potential clients another way.

Here is an example from my own recent projects. I wrote and published *The Parent's Guide to Facebook*. But before I did, I reached out to influencers and potential reviewers using the 'Strategic Friending Formula.' That is, I simply went into the Facebook search bar and typed "parents" or "parenting" into the bar and came up with a list of groups that have 'parent' in their name:

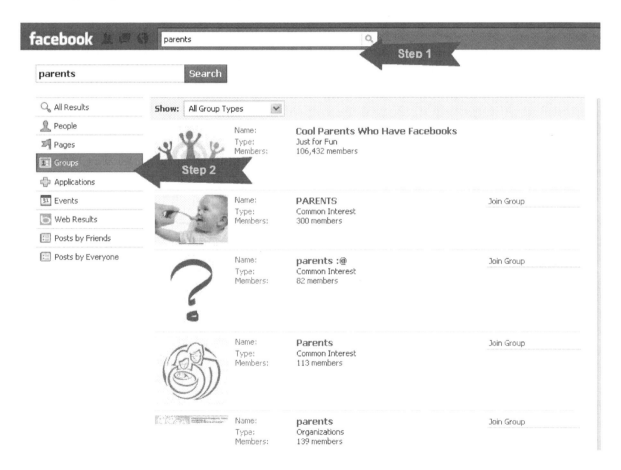

I then went into the groups and found the name of the

'Administrator' of the group. I joined the group and sent a personal message to the group administrator and officer stating with, " Dear _____, I just joined your group and have also written a new book that helps parents protect their children's privacy online. I would love to connect with you here on Facebook and offer you the opportunity to review my book. Best, Kathryn Rose."

I also performed an Internet search of top mom bloggers and came up with a list of the top 50. I then searched for them in Facebook, came across their profiles and sent them friend requests and/or messages asking for them to review my book and for feedback. (Note:, I DID NOT ask them to buy the book or sell it, simply to review it).

Guess what? I only had one person not respond to my request, and the ones who did respond reviewed it and published the review on their blog, which led to PR opportunities and sales of my books.

The other way to 'strategically friend' is find to find influencers and/or potential partners. For *Facebook Guide for Parents*, I looked for influencers who were involved in areas of interest to my potential readers, such as the Mommy blogger community, the parent-teacher organizations, and people who work to prevent cyber-bullying. Those folks became advocates for my book as well. Additionally, I found people with complementary products – e.g., a woman who has come up with an audio series that counsels parents of teens to help them through those tough years. She received my friend request, and then she called me on the phone! That led the parenting expert to review and recommend my book as well as sell it through her channels.

So let me review the strategic friending strategy. Follow these simple steps:

1. Identify your target audience.

2. Either type individual names of people or keywords into the Facebook search bar. Also search Google

and Linkedin to find names of potential future Facebook friends.

3. Identify groups and potential influencers.

4. Search for them on Facebook and send them a friend request – but ALWAYS include a personal note and let them know why you want to 'friend' them.

Please do not misunderstand. I do not advocate 'poaching' other people's friends or group members. This is a simple business tool, just as though you were at a networking function and you were looking for people you could speak with or meet that would further your business interests. Don't abuse the formula, but use it to connect with your target audience.

Chapter 11 - Creating Friend Lists

Now that you have all of these friends, and influencers, how do you keep them organized so you can market to them? Facebook provides an ideal solution for this within your profile: Friend Lists.

For example, you can create a group, or list, that contains your family members, another list for your friends from a book club, a list that has business contacts, and yet another one that has all your friends from a particular networking group.

> ➤ **You can place any contact into multiple Friend Lists.**
> ➤ **You can have an unlimited number of Friend Lists.**
> ➤ **Each Friend List can have a different privacy setting.**

Creating Friend Lists:

Go to 'Account' and click on 'Edit Friends.' This will bring up the list of all your current Facebook friends.

You will be able to create a new Friend List by clicking on the 'Create a List' link at the top of the page.

When you click on the 'Create New List' link, a window will pop up asking you to name your list. Give your new list a descriptive name to help you identify it later. The search box in the upper right allows you to search through your friends to find the people you want to add to the new list.

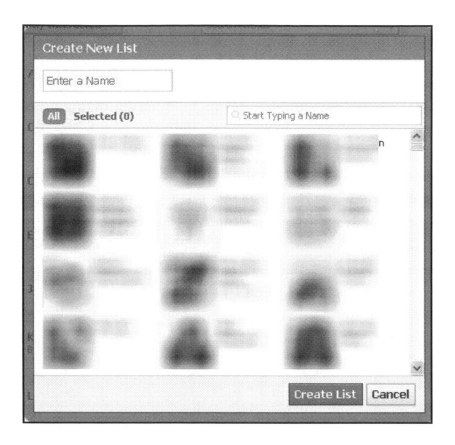

Clicking on a friend's name or picture will add them to the list, and you will see a blue box with a checkmark around it to indicate that you have successfully selected this person as a member of this new list.

You can name your list whatever you like: Key contacts, Business Contacts, Family, Friends, etc. When you're done selected friends for your list, click 'Create List' to complete the process. This List is now added to your master directory of 'Lists.'

Using Friend Lists:

You can create as many friend lists as you wish. Facebook offers you to sort your 'News Feed' to either 'Top News' or 'Most Recent.' As you can see, if you click on the drop down menu next to 'Most Recent,' your lists

will show up; you can now view your status updates sorted by lists.

Once a list is selected, you will only see the updates from the people in that list in the in the newsfeed area. So any time you want to check in with that group, you could do so very easily from your news feed, without having to sort through several other posts.

The other way to use the lists is in setting your profile privacy settings. Remember the 'Customize' option when setting up your privacy settings?

You can see here that 'Specific People' allows you to 'Enter a Name or a List.'

You can even use friend lists when you do status updates. This is a great feature if you only want to send certain status updates to certain people. For example, if you are a Realtor™, you may only want to share new listings with folks on your 'Prospects' list and not with your mom and aunt. It is very simple to share certain things with certain people:

On the 'what's on your mind' area, there is a little icon of a lock.

Here, you can click 'Customize' and then 'Specific People.' You can then send your status update only to the folks on that list.

Custom Privacy

✓ **Make this visible to**

These people: [Specific People... ▾]

[Key contacts ✕]

Only the people above can see this.

✕ **Hide this from**

These people: [Enter a Name or List]

☐ Make this my default setting   [Save Setting] [Cancel]

If you are using a particular list for your business the majority of the time, you can 'Make this your default setting' on the bottom left of the 'Custom Privacy' box, so you only have to change it when you decide to send out a personal message to close friends and family members.

Chapter 12 - The Wall

Your 'Wall' is the space on your Profile page that allows friends to post messages, to write notes to you, and it is the space where you can write posts by simply creating a 'Status Update.'

Each message on your wall is stamped with the time and date when the message was written. Your wall is visible to your friends. Different users' wall posts show up in the News Feed area. Your News Feed (visible if you click on the 'Home' link at the top of your page in the blue bar) is a collection of your friends' posts. The News Feed is Facebook's listing of posts by your friends. As I mentioned in a previous chapter, there are two options for viewing posts in your News Feed:

1. **Top News** is selected by Facebook and shows the posts from your friends that Facebook thinks are most interesting to you based on your recent activity and interactions.

2. **Most Recent** is an actual real time chronological listing of your friends latest posts presented in the 'live' stream of updates. If you have established friend lists, click on the arrow next to 'Most Recent' and then you can sort posts by 'Friend Lists.'

You can toggle back and forth to show posts from 'Top News' or 'Most Recent.'

Many users leave short messages and notes on their friends' walls to stay in touch. You can attach links to websites they may be interested in or post photos they may enjoy. This is how you can keep in contact with your friends and stay current on their lives. You can post replies to their status updates to engage in conversation. Again, don't post anything that you want to be private.

Private interaction is done through Messages. Messages are visible only to the sender and recipient of the Message, similar to email.

You can access Messages by clicking on the 'Messages' icon in the blue menu bar, or in the left menu selection under your profile I.D. on the 'Home' page.

Chapter 13 - Adding Photos

One of the most popular applications on Facebook is the Photos application. The main features of this application are:

> **Upload unlimited numbers of photos.**

> **Create photo albums.**

> **Post comments on photos and albums.**

> **Privacy settings for individual albums, limiting the groups of users who can see an album. For example, the privacy of an album can be set so that only the user's friends can see the album, while the privacy of another album can be set so that all Facebook users can see it.**

You can find Photos by clicking on the 'Photos' link in the left menu bar of the 'Profile' page. Click on upload photos to upload a new photo or album. Or in your own photo array, you will see that each photo is tagged by its name.

If you already uploaded an album or a photo, click on the name, and then you will see an option to 'Edit Album,' located on the left site. Click on 'Edit Album Info' and be taken to a screen where you can make privacy adjustments (photo below).

You can 'customize' privacy settings for each of your photos and/or for entire albums.

Edit Album - Kat's Photos

| Edit Photos | Add More | Organize | Edit Info | Delete |

Back to Album

Album Name: Kat's Photos

Location:

Description:

Privacy: 🔒 Who can see this?

Only Friends ▾

Everyone
Friends of Friends
Only Friends
Customize...

Save Changes   Cancel

You also have the ability to 'Tag' or label people in a photo. For instance, if a photo features one of your Facebook friends, you can tag or identify that friend in the photo. This sends a notification to that friend, telling them they have been tagged, and it provides them with a link to see the photo.

To 'Tag' someone in a photo, just click on their face. A square will appear framing your friend's face and a box will appear that says "type any name or tag." Start typing a friend's name and Facebook will begin to offer you auto-fill choices.

When your friends are tagged in your photo, they will receive the notification that they have been tagged in a photo, including a link to view the photo. They will have the option to 'Remove Tag' if they don't want to be identified.

Chapter 14 - Creating a Facebook Group

In early October 2010, Facebook introduced a new group feature. Similar to friend lists, this new Facebook 'group' feature allows you to group just some close friends, business associates, employees or whomever you would like and communicate just with that group. This is a basic overview as this is a new feature and will most likely undergo some changes.

To create a Facebook Group, go to the 'Groups' icon, located in the left menu bar of your 'Home' page.

From here, you can search for groups and also create a new group. To create your own group, click on 'Groups' and then on '+ Create a Group.'

Groups   + Create a Group

Groups
Share, chat, and email with small groups of friends.

How will you use g
- Share baby photos w
- Create shared docs f
- Chat with all the mem

Create Group

Chat as a group
Talk to group members in real time, or catch up with the conversation later.

Connect over email
Send and receive updates using the group email address, just like a mailing list.

For more information, read the Top Questions About Groups.

A box will then pop up. Enter the name of your group and then the friends you want to add in your group.

Remember, you can add only your Facebook friends in the group you are creating. Type the names in the **Members** box (no need to type full name, as after typing the initials, Facebook automatically displays your friend's name).

After typing all the names, choose the privacy level. For example, you can choose to have your group 'closed'; therefore, all the members will be public (anyone on Facebook can see them) but the content will be private.

Your Facebook group has now been created. Just a reminder: be aware that the members of the group are PUBLIC but depending upon how you have the settings configured, the group content may be private.

The 'Groups' feature is an 'opt-out,' meaning anyone can create a group with you in it, and you will have to remove yourself if you do not want to be in the group.

The interesting thing about this new feature is that you can chat as a group. The "chat" feature is an instant message type feature in Facebook.

You will also at some point be able to share your status updates with just these folks in your group, which is, again, similar to Facebook Friend lists.

To edit your group once it is set up click on the group title, then go to the right of the screen.

Then click 'Edit Group.' Next, you can change the name, the privacy settings and you can even set up an email address for your group that will allow you to communicate with the group even if you are not logged in to Facebook.

Test ▸ Basic Information   ◄ Back to Group

Group Name: [▼] Test

Privacy: 🔒 Closed ▼   Members are public, content is private

Email Address: Choose for Group

Description:

Save Changes   Cancel

Chapter 15 - Create Your Business Page

One of the greatest benefits of Business Facebook Pages is that it encourages user-generated content. People who 'like' your page, can participate in discussions, share videos, photos & links, post on the wall, leave comments, and share information from your page with their friends via a 'Share' button. This creates buzz around your business page, increases your online visibility and promotes your brand.

Another benefit of a Business Page is that all the interactions that people have with your page will enter their live feed and therefore become visible to all of their friends. When someone 'likes' or becomes a 'fan' of your Business Page, they can also suggest to their friends that they should consider liking or becoming a fan. This can create a 'viral' effect, helping to expose your brand to more people.

The most important benefit of Facebook pages needs repeating at this point, to make sure you understand the role it plays in an online visibility strategy for your business:

Facebook Pages are public profiles and therefore indexed by Google. This is the most important benefit to having a business presence on Facebook, as online visibility is crucial to creating a competitive advantage for your business. If I haven't convinced you yet, let me just reiterate from the first chapter that more than 10 million users 'Like' Facebook Pages each and every day. In doing so, they make those brand names visible to all of their friends. Facebook is thus also an important search engine and your business needs to be searchable and visible there.

For some reason, Facebook does not make creating a page very obvious or intuitive. This may be because the original idea was to use Facebook to connect with friends and family and that using Facebook for business is relatively new. Businesses, however, saw an amazing opportunity in what Facebook was offering and embraced the social marketing model with great eagerness. Soon, success stories were created and now major corporations like Coke, Walmart, Starbucks and Dunkin Donuts created fan pages. So let's start right now to create your success story.

To create a new Business Page, start from your 'Home' page. Click on 'Ads and Pages' on the left hand side of your Wall.

Or click on the 'Advertising' link, located all the way down on the right hand side of the page, in the footer area.

Select 'Pages' and then click on '+ Create Page.'

Take a look at the 'Create a Page' options. On this screen, you can choose what type of business you are setting up the page for.

Before deciding, please take a look at all options and make sure to choose the one that will best fit with your business. There are slightly different nuances for each type of page. For instance, if you set up a page for a store, you will get a space to enter store hours. You can set it up as a brand product or organization, or as an artist, band or public figure. It is important to mention that you should never set up a page for a business unless you've been authorized to do so or are the business owner or representative.

Another important step is to choose the name for your page. You can change it later (only if fewer than 100 people like your page); so try to consider a few things when naming your page:

> **How well does the name match what you do? Does it describe the products or services you're offering, or**

does it suggest the value you are creating for your customers.

➢ Does it contain your keywords?

➢ Is it easy to remember? Make it easy for people to remember the name, and, therefore, to find you with minimal effort.

➢ Make sure you spell it correctly.

➢ Make a list of 4-5 names for your page and ask someone who knows your business to help you evaluate them.

➢ Be happy with your decision.

➢ In case you make a mistake, don't sweat it. You cannot change the name, but you can delete the page and start over.

➢ What you are creating here is an extension to your website that is simpler but potentially even more visible.

Chapter 16 - Editing Your Fan Page

Now that you have chosen a name and completed the process, now is time to edit your page and provide information about your business.

I'll now cover the steps recommended by Facebook; then I will make some recommendations of my own.

Step 1: Upload an image. The image that you will upload here may be your picture, your logo, or a combination of the two in one image. The dimensions should be within these parameters: 180 pixels wide by 540 pixels long. You have done this before with your profile picture; so just follow the same steps.

The other thing I want to mention is that when you set up this image, Facebook will ask you to pick a thumbnail or small segment of this picture that will appear as your page's avatar. This will be your visual representation every time you post on your page, and it will go out in your fans' news feeds as well. Unless you are design savvy, it is a good idea to invest in the services of a graphic designer to put something together that is a good representation of your company. For example if your company name is Rose-Smith Accounting, maybe the thumbnail can be RS or some other symbol that your organization would like to be identified with. It's okay to upload a temporary image and then change it later, when you have a better idea of what you want it to be. But do not leave the picture area blank.

Step 2: Invite friends. This is one of the reasons it is so important to try to use your Facebook personal profile as a business resource. You can easily invite people to like your page, but only if you are friends with them first. If you took the time to set up friend lists, you can easily invite just those who pertain to your business. I recommend that you skip this step until your page is complete.

Step 3: Tell your fans. This is a cool new feature offered by Facebook. You can 'Invite' friends to fan your page by sending them an email. You can import your contact database to Facebook for sending out an email. I feel it is borderline spam but I know some who have used it with great success. Just be sure to import your own contacts and contacts you really believe would be interested in your page.

Step 4: Post a status update. You are not even close to ready to do this yet. So let's get the page set up and then we'll talk about how to craft updates.

Step 5: Promote this page on your website. You can create a 'Like' box or widget for your page so folks can easily 'Like' you even, if they are not on the Facebook site.

Step 6: Set up your mobile phone. This step I recommend you take the time to complete at this point. This is a very useful feature if you're on the road a lot. You can send updates to a page-specific email box and post photos and videos to your page. Also, you can set it up so that you can update your fan page status directly from your mobile phone.

Now that I've covered Facebook's recommended steps, here are a few that I would recommend.

Be sure to click on 'Info' and add the information about your organization.

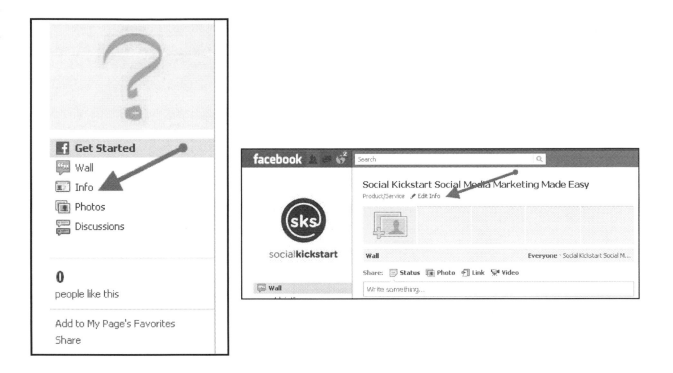

To add information about your page, either click on the
'Info' area underneath the profile picture or 'Edit Info" at
the top of the page. Once you click on the 'Edit Info' link,
you will come to this screen:

Let's start from the top: Category. Double check this and change it if for some reason you selected the wrong category when you set up the page.

Username: you will be able to set up a unique URL username when you reach 25 fans. I go into more detail about usernames in chapter 20.

Page name: if your page has fewer than 100 fans, you can change the name.

The rest of this area is self-explanatory. As you fill it out, be sure your fans (as most of us still call people who 'like' pages), know what it is that you do or offer. Make sure your unique selling proposition (USP) is obvious. Be transparent, focus on your value proposition, and be creative. Also, make sure to include a live, clickable URL (using the http://) not just the 'www' in the website area.

Now we'll move on to editing the fan page and adding information.

On the business or fan page, click on 'Edit Page.' Here, you will be able to configure your page and add additional information.

Social Kickstart Social Media Marketing Made Easy
Product/Service ✏ Edit Info   Edit Page

From the top of the right menu, we will cover the different areas of the Facebook fan page:

Your settings:

As I mentioned in the beginning of this book, Facebook changed the way pages interact with other pages inside the platform. You can now comment on your own page as you would comment on other brand pages.

This first area 'Posting Preferences' covers how you want to post to your own page. If you "always post on my page as (brand)," selected, posts that you make on your page will come up with your logo and your brand. If you uncheck this, posts will show on your page with your photo as if you posted from your personal page.

Next area: email notifications. You can set these up so
you get an email notification (to your personal email
account) every time someone posts on your page. This is
a great feature for you to keep in constant contact with
your fan base.

Manage Permissions

On this screen you can configure some of the
functionality of your page. Before you get started, I
recommend that you make sure to check off 'only admins

can see this page' so you have time to work on the page before anyone can interact with it. Be sure to click on 'Save Changes' to make sure the settings are saved. Once your page is set up properly, you can come back here and uncheck the box to make your page public.

In this area you can also set up country restrictions. Let's say you only want to do business in Canada – as perhaps you have a franchise and are restricted from doing business in another country. If you leave this blank, it defaults to all countries.

If your product has adult content or is alcohol-related, there may be some age restrictions you would set; you can put these here.

The next area refers to 'Wall' settings. This is where you control the interaction that takes place on your page. Many times, when folks ask me to look at their pages, I notice that this setting is set for 'only posts by page.' This restricts people who come to your fan page from interacting with you and your brand. This may deter them from becoming a fan of your page (or 'liking' your page); so I always recommend that you set this to 'Everyone.' Activity between your brand and your fans increases your visibility.

The next area on this screen is the 'default landing tab.' There is a way within Facebook to set up special 'tabs' seen on the left side of the business page, similar to pages on a website. I recommend that you consider setting up some custom tabs for your page. When you do this, this setting is what is used so that anyone who is not yet a fan of your page or has not yet clicked 'Like' will land on the tab of your choice. You may want that to be your 'info tab.' I recommend that you create a custom 'welcome tab'

Posting ability: I suggest that you allow fans to write notes, post on your wall, and upload photos or videos to your page to encourage fan interaction. You, as an administrator, can always delete content that you do not want there.

'Moderation Blocklist and Profanity Blocklist': In this area, content can be entered and if anyone tries to post on your wall with words that are entered here, the posts are not shown on the wall. This is a great feature, but it doesn't always work. I recommend that you set this up but that you don't count on it to run automatically. Nothing replaces a human being's watchful eye.

Basic Information

This is the same screen we saw earlier when setting up the page. This information will be located on the 'Info' tab of your page.

Profile Picture

You can add or upload a profile picture here. Also be sure to select 'edit thumbnail' and adjust the image. The thumbnail is how your image will appear in the newsfeeds around the site.

Featured

You can 'Like' other pages, whose thumbnails will be displayed on the lower left side of your page. You can also show page owners (admins) pictures if you would like.

Marketing

Here you can create an advertisement for your page, get a page 'badge' to post on your website or create a 'Like' button to add to your website. I recommend that you put this on hold until you are finished setting up your page.

Manage Admins

In this area you can decide who you would like to be an administrator of your page. Be very careful here: admins have the power to communicate with your fans as if they were YOU. Also, they have the power to delete your fan page completely. Only make someone an admin if they are responsible and trustworthy. You can only make someone an admin if you are Facebook friends with them.

Social Kickstart Social Media Marketing Made Easy

‹ View Page

Manage Permissions
Basic Information
Profile Picture
Marketing
Manage Admins
Applications
Mobile
Insights →
Pages Help →

Kathryn Rose

Start typing a name or email...   Remove

Add another admin

Save Changes   Cancel

Applications

There are countless applications you can add to your page to create a custom user experience. In the beginning of setting up your page, Facebook provides some default applications for you. Also, depending upon what type of page you have set up, Facebook will also suggest relevant applications.

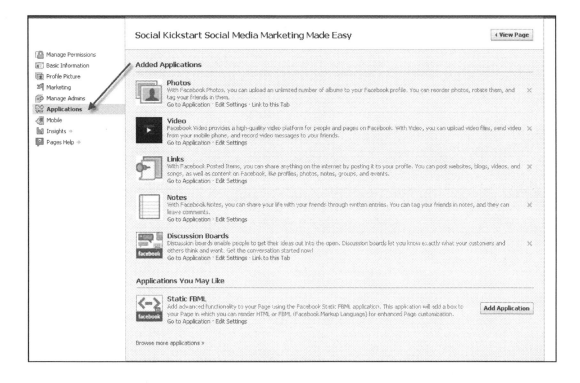

Below I will cover some of the main page applications :

Uploading Photos, Videos and Links

It is very easy to attach a link or upload a photo or video. The first step is to write something in the status update box, then click on the top row 'photo' or 'link' or 'video.' And then you either attach a link or upload the photo or video from your computer.

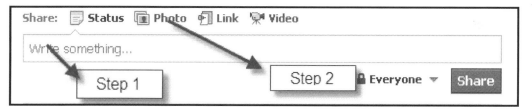

If you would like to upload a video from YouTube, go to YouTube, copy the link and attach it as a link.

When you attach a link, pick the thumbnail image (if applicable) that you want to show next to the link or a

description paragraph by clicking on the left or right arrow (next to 'Choose a Thumbnail'). If you do not find a suitable image, cheeck the 'No Thumbnail' box; then click 'Share.' I recommend that you pick a thumbnail because it looks more engaging on the page. If possible, try not to put the link into the post; attach any links instead. It looks cleaner and more professional.

A note about photos: on Facebook pages, much like your personal profile page, Facebook displays the last 5 photos that the page has uploaded along the top of the page. Pictures that others upload to your page are not displayed on the top of the profile.

Notes

There are two options with the 'Notes' application:

1. Create your own blog-like post with this application. (If you have a blog, you can import it easily to your Fan Page, either through the 'Notes' application or the 'Networked Blogs' application.)

Go to the 'Notes' application page and click on the RSS
feed symbol; here, just follow the instructions.

Discussion Board

Don't discount the Discussion Board. Although it doesn't

draw the eye as much as the Wall does, it's an effective

tool to keep conversations going. Wall posts can get lost

in the stream. Discussion boards are like forums and are the perfect space to offer your Fans a way to stay connected to each other.

Create discussions by setting specific topics that will engage your fans in conversations with you (through your page) and with each other. This way, your page will become another desirable destination place for like-minded individuals and will encourage them to return often.

Mobile

I covered some of this in the beginning of the chapter. If you have not set up your mobile device, I recommend that you do so. You can set it up so that you can update your fan page status directly from your mobile phone.

This area gives you many options for interacting with your page via a mobile phone.

Once you are happy with all of your set up tabs, your next step is to 'Publish This Page.' Either go back to the manage permissions area or click 'View page' and click 'Publish this Page.'

As soon as it is published, you'll want to 'Like' your own page. By liking your page, Facebook will send an automatic notification to all your friends, telling them that you have 'Liked' the page, and it will list the page name. This notification enters the News Feed and becomes a potentially viral piece of information, encouraging your friends to check out your new page.

In addition, you will want to go back to your fan page and click 'Suggest to Friends.'

This will bring up a list of your friends. You can now invite them to become fans or to 'Like' your page. Now, if you followed the guides from earlier chapters when setting up 'Friend lists,' this process will be much easier for you. Simply click on the 'Filter Friends' area and click on the name of the list. You will still have to invite each friend individually, but it will save you some time.

Chapter 17: Using Facebook as Your Page

You can now use Facebook as your business page. What does that mean? You can post on other business pages in such a way that your brand image is displayed instead of your personal photo. Many of my clients love this feature because they are now allowed to communicate as an organization rather than simply as a person to clients and prospective clients. For example, if I see someone asking a question about social media on their page, I can comment as the Social Kickstart page. That way, they interact with me as if I am a company, or brand. This is also useful when you have other employees who are administrators of your page. In the past, if an admin of your page posted on another page, it would be their picture that showed up. Now, they can log in as a page and send and receive communications as a company or brand, represented by that page. You cannot 'Friend' people as a page however.

A word of caution: Do not use this tactic to spam other pages. You wouldn't run into Starbucks and hand out Dunkin Donuts coupons, right? The same is true for Facebook. I would not go on another social media training page and post an answer to a question that one of their fans asked, representing my page or myself. It's just not the right thing to do. If a page posts spam on your page, simply go to the right of the post, click the 'x' and say 'remove post and ban page;' that page can then never come back again.

To 'login as page' you can either go to the 'Account' area on the top right of your screen and click 'Use Facebook as Page.'

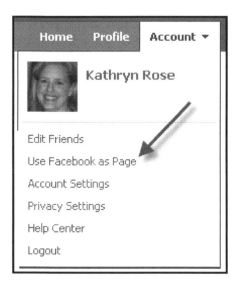

Or, you can go to the page and click 'Use Facebook as (brand),' located under the pictures of the admins of the page on the upper right side.

Use Facebook as Social Kickstart Social Media Marketing Made Easy

Promote with an Ad

View Insights

Suggest to Friends

Chapter 18 - Fan Page Strategy

Now that you've set up your page, let's talk about strategy. In developing a STRATEGY for using Facebook for your business, ask yourself these two questions.

1. What do I want to share about my brand? What is my USP, or Unique Selling Proposition? What is it about my business, products or services that positions me above my competition? The clearer your message, the easier it is to be kept TOP of MIND.

2. How can I effectively communicate your brand message on Facebook?

Remember, more than 10 million people 'Like' pages every day. This is a beautiful number. When people like your Page, their friends see your Page name, and your brand spreads organically and possibly virally throughout many networks of like-minded and potentially new customers.

I recommend another key visibility strategy: connect with influencers in your industry with whom you have a relationship. Invite them to join your Page. Ask if they would be willing to recommend your page to their fans or even become administrators of your Group or Fan Page, so that they can invite their friends.

What do you post to attract Fans and keep them Engaged?

Post industry news, tips, events in your industry, resources and links to articles that your page subscribers would appreciate. Add links to articles, photos. A great way to share dynamic content from a variety of media is by posting links, photos and videos. You can post links to websites, blogs, videos, music, and a variety of other content on Facebook. All you have to do is enter the valid URL (formatted like: http:// for it to be clickable).

You can even send out updates to SPECIFIC fans, much like you did on your personal profile when you created friend lists.

When creating status updates for your page, click on the lock next to the 'Share' button and then click 'Customize.'

From here you can select 'Location' or even 'Language.'

When you click on 'Location,' enter a country or a specific city location.

- Post at least one question a day to encourage engagement. Make it short. You're allowed 420 characters per post, but I find posts at around 200 characters are most effective. You can also use polls to create fun interactivity.

- Encourage your Fans to share what you've written on their own page to increase your visibility with their friends. Polls are also a great way to crowdsource topics your Fans are looking to learn more about. Help them discover which product or service can answer the needs they express. An eager audience leads to more sales. Threadless.com is a perfect example of a company who has mastered the art of crowdsourcing. 'Polls' is the name of an actual application you can add to your page.

- Offer help. I posted an offer to give feedback on one of my client's pages and received more than 100 requests for help. This was a great way to provide value and spread the word about the client's page.

- Get personal. Address your Fans as if you were talking to one fan at a time: "We'd love your feedback. What do you find is the most effective strategy for saving money? What is your favorite city for business or pleasure travel?"

  This way of formulating your questions makes them more personal, and it forms a stronger bond with your fans by making them feel included in your community.

By following these strategies, your fan page will grow exponentially.

Interacting & Engaging

Be interesting, but most of all be interested in people and their needs. People like pages to stay connected, and the like to receive insider information and offers and to learn more about your topic.

If you've just created your Page, post at least once a day. As your Fan base grows, you'll want to post a few more times each day. Be considerate and only post information related to your topic, industry and Fan base.

If a Fan posts something on your wall, or responds to your post, thank them by name and reply promptly. Also keep in mind when the high usage windows are; your fans will most likely be on Facebook early morning, lunch time and early evenings.

Tag people in your posts. Type in the @ symbol and then, without a space, start typing in the desired name and select the correct one from the drop down box.

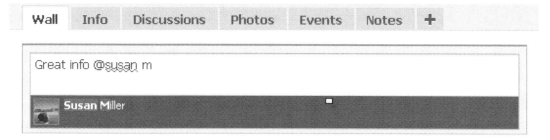

Once selected, the name will appear in blue, making it an active link. You can tag up to six identities per post. By tagging in your post, the post will also appear on your friends Wall, Fan Page Wall as well as your fans' NewsFeeds. You can also tag events and other Fan Pages; this means more visibility for your Fan Page. Keep in mind that you must be friends with the person you are tagging, or a Fan of the page you're tagging. Also, this is not a new feature, but it is still a little spotty in terms of when it works and when it doesn't. But it's a good strategy, nonetheless, and it's one you should get used to using – particularly for connecting with industry leaders or high visibility friends and fans. Your post will show up on their wall and in their friends' news streams and thereby act as an advertisement for you and your business. Use this strategy wisely to provide value to your business profile. Don't spam.

Chapter 19 - Creating Events on your Page

Another way to engage with your audience is to create events. You can create an event announcement for your teleseminars, webinars, networking meetings, parties, sales or any other organized gathering and let your friends and fans know about it.

Click on 'Events' on the left side of the screen. If you do not see events listed, go to the 'Edit Page' area, click on the 'Apps' tab on the left, find the events app and click on 'Edit Settings.' Then click 'Add' to tab.

This process is true for every application you add. If it does not show up automatically on the wall area, you will have to add it manually. Also, you can reorder the wall application list.

To do so, go to the bottom of the list and click 'Edit.' Then you simply click on the application and drag it to your chosen location. You cannot change the order of the 'Wall' and 'Info' areas, however.

To create an event, follow the on-screen, step-by-step instructions on how to create an event and invite your community members (Friends) to join you and to participate.

Create an Event

When?	Today	7:00 pm ⌄	Add end time
What are you planning?			
Where?			
	Add street address		
More info?			
Who's invited?	**Select Guests**		
	☑ Show the guest list on the event page		
	☑ Non-admins can write on the wall		
	Create Event		

Events have three different privacy options:

1. **Open**: Anyone can add themselves to the guest list without receiving an invitation or being approved by an admin. They can see the event information and all associated content (photos, Wall posts and videos).

2. **Closed**: People must be invited to be on the guest list. Everyone can see the event info. and request an invitation from the admin. Only those people who have received an invitation can see the event Wall and photos. People who are not invited will not see stories about closed events.

3. **Secret**: The event cannot be found in searches. These events are by invite only. People who have not been invited cannot view any of the event info.

Chapter 20 - Promoting Your Page

People can elect to 'Like' your Page, but only if they know about it. So you need to make an effort to introduce people to your Page and to your company, and to be consistent and persistent in that effort.

As I mentioned, one way of letting your Facebook friends know about your Page is to INVITE them to 'Like' your Page. You can send your personal profile friends a short note explaining what your page is all about and why you would like them to visit it, to post a comment and to become a fan. You can do this by sending them a private message through Facebook. Make sure to include your page's full URL, so that they can just click and visit.

The other way is to enlist the help of your friends. You can ask your friends or your fans to help get the word out by suggesting your page to *their* friends.

All they have to do is go to your page and click on the

'Suggest to Friends' link and then select their friends.

The most important part of promoting your Facebook Page is to be available, engaging and consistent with your posts. Post regularly, answer Fan's posts and comments, create interesting and useful content, and share valuable information. Make sure to promote your page by including the clickable link to your page on your website, your blog, your other social network profiles, and your email signature.

Another great strategy is a press release. When I talk about press releases, I don't mean the traditional kind that is meant to get you featured in the newspaper. I am talking about online press releases that are meant to drive traffic and to place strategic URLs for Google and other search engines. There are a few free press release sites I use, and they syndicate throughout the Internet.

Remember to use keywords and to put the live clickable link (with the http://) in the release. Here is a list of the free sites I use:

http://prlog.com
http://pr.com
http://pr-inside.com
http://free-press-release.com

Creating a Unique Page URL

The real power of Facebook Pages starts once you have reached your first milestone of having 25 fans. The power of authority of Facebook's URL is in being number two in search engine rankings. **When your name, or company name is a part of that URL, you gain the power of Facebook's search engine rankings as well.**

As of this writing, Facebook allows you to create a unique page URL that will look like this:
http://facebook.com/**google**

Yes, even Google has a Facebook fan page! You can use your unique user name in your marketing communications, company website and business cards.

Go to the 'basic information' section of the 'Edit Page' area and click on the link there. Be sure to think this through because once you have a URL it cannot be changed later.

Having your vanity URL creates better brand visibility when you share it with your community and folks OFF LINE as well. You can add this to your business cards, brochures, radio spots, newspaper ads or any business touchpoint.

It's best that you create a username that is straightforward and easy to remember. Facebook encourages you to consider the following when creating a username for Pages:

> Create a username that is close to your business name.

- Usernames can only contain alphanumeric characters.
- Choose a username you will be happy with for the long term. Usernames are not transferable.
- Once you set up your username it cannot be changed.
- Your <u>profile</u> username and your <u>page</u> username cannot be the same.

Promote your page on your website with a box or widget from the 'Marketing' area of the 'Edit Page' section. This is simply a piece of code you or your webmaster can install on your business website. Go to the 'Edit Page' area, then click on promote with a 'Like' box.

Clicking here will bring you to a page where you can create different kinds of badges. Once you have selected a badge for your site, click 'copy code' and post or give to your web person to post to your website.

Also be sure to cross promote your Fan page across all social media platforms. Tell your Twitter followers, blog readers, LinkedIn connections, and ask them to help you spread the word. When you position your page as a resource to help people, then your friends, followers and connections are more likely to share.

Stay connected with your Fans by going beyond the page and sending updates with a call to action. Example: save 10% today with coupon code XYZ.

Promote your page via Facebook Ads

Facebook ads are a highly targeted and inexpensive way to promote your page. Here are some tips to help you succeed with a Facebook ad campaign.

To place an ad on Facebook, go to the left side of your newsfeed area and click on 'Ads and Pages.' On the next screen click 'Create an Ad."

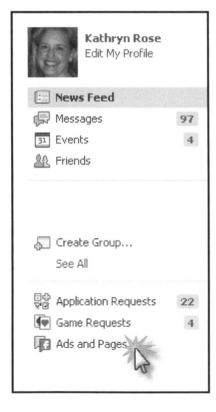

AD TITLE - Your ad needs a title; maximum 25 characters. Make sure it catches people's attention!

AD COPY - The copy of your ad is limited to 135 characters. Be simple and direct to get your point across while stating the call to action. Are you offering a coupon, promo gift? Needless to say, be concise as 135 characters, including spaces, goes quickly. There's a lot of competition out there, so be sure to stand out. If your goal is brand/company name recognition, I suggest using your company name in the ad title or somewhere in the copy of the ad.

There are many **rules Facebook** has laid out about best practices when creating ads; so let's review those now.

KISS – Keep it simple; no run on sentences. Use correct grammar and use no appreciations or acronyms unless they represent the name of the company. Use proper spacing, commas and periods. Leave out the dramatic symbols!!! No chat language accepted here.

SHORT – Be concise and keep the details for your landing page, website, product description page clear. Your GOAL is to catch the potential fan's eye and get them to click on your ad.

CALL TO ACTION – Your ad should express your call to action. Do you want them to buy something, learn something, or attend an event? Spell out exactly what you are offering.

LANDING PAGE – Your ad must be relevant to your landing page or else it will not be approved. In other words, if your ad is for a local restaurant and when the visitor clicks thru, they arrive at a website or Fan page which has nothing to do with dining or food, then your ad will be rejected by Facebook as misleading.

GET TO THE PAGE – Be sure to point the link to the page on your website or the tab on your Fan page that best complements the ad. The more clicks or time it takes a visitor to find the relevant page, the more likely she or he is to get annoyed and leave without 'Liking' or viewing your landing page. So, if your offer is a particular product that is three pages deep into your website, point the ad to that specific page and not to your HOME page.

Facebook also has a list of Best Practices you can read in more detail. You'll see that link on the 'Create an Ad' page.

IMAGE – Facebook pages are already very busy looking

because Facebook is a social platform that includes images, videos and plenty or text from profiles, groups and Fan pages. You will want to find creative images that will grab the attention of users and make them *want* to click your ad. Your ad image will vary and will automatically be formatted to fit the appropriate specifications. There's no need on your part to format the picture to the required size. If there is text in your image, be sure that it is still legible when shrunk to ad size. You can use a stock photo you've purchased, one of your own photos or a graphic such as a logo as your image. You can even superimpose a message over your image to catch their attention before they've even had the chance to read the text. Be sure to select an eye-catching, relevant image that is appropriate. No nudity or embarrassing images. Facebook is very strict in ensuring that no one in their community is offended. Needless to say, ad titles or images that lean on a negative side to catch people's attention such as 'You're Fat' or 'You're Ugly' will never be approved.

TARGETING YOUR AD

Sit back for a moment and think of yourself as your ideal customer. When creating your ad, think about who would most likely purchase your product. Are you selling to a man or woman or maybe both? Do you know where they live, their age group, level or education, their likes, hobbies, interests? The more you know your customers, the better prepared you will be in creating your ad. If you have a clear vision of your ideal customer, you can create an ad to attract exactly that segment of the market. Take time to envision your ideal client profile. Be sure to stay on track and keep in mind target relevance. For example, if you are selling a book written in French, you'll get a better ROI if you target French speaking countries.

Facebook ads let you target viewers on a large or small scale. This is a very useful feature, so you don't waste time or money on ads that do not work. I also recommend 'split testing.' That is, designing several ads and running them simultaneously with different images, headlines and copy and keeping those that work and deleting those that don't. You can get started on Facebook ads with as little as $1 per day.

You can either pay for clicks or impressions. It depends upon your budget. I like to use the impressions, at least at first, for split testing.

> **Facebook says:** As an advertiser paying for **clicks (CPC)**, you are indicating that what is most important to you is driving traffic to a page on Facebook or your own website.

> As an advertiser paying for views (**impressions**) (CPM), you are indicating that it is most important for users to see your ad and your brand. You will want to focus on making your ad as clear and informative as possible and having your brand or company's name be easily recognized.

Making a decision on CPC vs. CPM is a tough one. Simply

put, there's no one form of successful bidding strategy on Facebook. You have to try both methods, test and test again.

CPC sounds great at first. You only pay for the clicks you receive. But the problem is, if you don't get a good click through rate, Facebook starts showing your ads less and less often. You could end up with zero impressions pretty quickly. This quickly kills many campaigns that may otherwise have been successful.

Chapter 21 - Page insights

Facebook Insights measures user exposure, actions, and behavior on your Facebook Page. By understanding activity and performance, as well as trends and comparisons, you can make better decisions in order to improve your business on Facebook and elsewhere. The Insights box is a free service for Facebook Pages. Only Page administrators can view this information. The insights area can be accessed by the right side of the page; click on 'view insights.'

These are screen shots from one of my clients (a major alcohol brand):

In this area, you can see the new 'Likes', total lifetime 'Likes' and the monthly active users.

High quality content will have interactive fan bases capable of virally spreading; therefore, the number of fans will grow with the popularity of your Page. When you create a post on your Page, it enters a News Feed that potentially drives a viral spreading of information on Facebook through networks of friends.

You can also see such things in this area as the breakdown of fans by demographics (e.g., age, gender, geography). You can also view what posts receive the most interaction, and what tabs fans are landing on most, and so on.

Studying your Page Insight graphs can help you improve the quality of posts, so that you can create better interactions with your community and harness the power of any viral information spread.

Chapter 22: Advanced Facebook Strategies

As the title of this book implies, this is more of a beginner's guide, but I would like to run through a couple of advanced strategies that you can use to enhance your Facebook experience.

Custom Tabs Using FBML or IFrames – FBML stands for "Facebook Mark-up Language." It is a proprietary code that is based mainly on HTML code, which is used in web pages. When you see custom tabs like "Contest" or "Welcome," these are designed in FBML . FBML tabs can make your page look more professional. You can add sign-up boxes for your email list, a "Follow me on Twitter" button, not to mention the ability to actually SELL from your Facebook page. These custom tabs need some advanced training to design, and there are many designers out there who have low fees and who can do a good job. As of this writing, Facebook has announced that they will be doing away with FBML and going to all I-frames sometime in early 2011; this means that eventually you may need a specialist to do these pages. They have said that they would "grandfather" in any FBML pages that exist.

A great tool for designing custom tabs is http://lujure.com, created by my friend Nathan Latka. There is a free option that you can try.

Time Saving Tools – you can connect your Facebook account with your Twitter account easily by going to http://facebook.com/twitter and selecting the appropriate account. Another great tool is Hootsuite http://hootsuite.com, which allows the management of all of your social networks in one place. They also have a free version for you if you are managing just your own networks.

Facebook Places – similar to Foursquare and Gowalla, Facebook Places launched in August of 2010. Facebook says: Facebook Places provides a presence for your business's physical store locations, encouraging your customers to share that they visited your business by "check-in" to your place. As of this writing, this feature is only available on the I-phone, but I suspect that the blackberry and android versions are not far behind.

Using the Facebook Page "photo" area as a promotional tool

With the recent change to the look of the business pages, like personal profiles, there are 5 photos displayed across the top of the page. Follow these instructions and you will be able to use them for marketing purposes. (I want to give credit to my friend Mari Smith for alerting me to this idea.)

Here is an example from one of my clients, Voices of September 11.

VOICES of September 11th

Non-Profit Organization · New Canaan, CT ✎ Edit Info

Wall   Everyone · VOICES of September 11th

Share: 📝 **Status** 🖼 **Photo** 🔗 **Link** 📹 **Video**

Write something...

If you click on the photo, a 'lightbox' comes up:

And below the picture, there is a link that leads to the donation page.

How you do this is by finding an image, and using photoshop or some other kind of photo software. Add the call to action to the image, make the image 970x680 (Facebook resizes it to fit the picture window), add the 'caption,' which is your call to action and a link (complete with the http://) and then upload to the page. If you are doing a number of these, you will want to first make your page invisible to its fans. This way, when the photos post to the wall, the fans don't get notified. You can then remove the post from the wall and you will see that your photo ad remains on the page. Voila! You can stop by and donate to Voices – they do good work!

Facebook Checklist For Success

☐ Create your Daily Activity Facebook Plan.
Most people are like you: too busy to dedicate several hours per day to Facebook. But in order to create a good presence and strong connections, you will have to schedule some Facebook time every day.

☐ Every morning, set aside about 15-20 minutes to have a cup of coffee/tea with Facebook. You will find it is a great way to start your day. Scheduling another 15-20 minutes in the evening or late afternoon to check in and interact will help you grow your community. Once you create this routine, you will enjoy spending quality time with your friends and fans.

☐ Create a list of on-going topics to discuss or post. This is an organic list that will change as you learn what your fans want. Your community will get to know you better when you establish consistency and also deliver valuable communication.

☐ Example list:

- ○ Give an expert tip.

- ○ Share something you've learned (mention the source/give credit/share a link), or ask a question about your community and their needs.

- ○ Ask or tell about events in your industry (local, live or virtual).

- ○ Share your personal interests or passions (an affirmation, motivational quote, or an anecdote)

Suggested morning Facebook activity

Schedule (15 min):

- ✓ Check birthdays, post happy birthday messages on friends' walls.

- ✓ Check your Wall for any posts by friends and reply to

any you see relevant and interesting.

- ✓ Connect with at least 4-5 people and comment on their posts.

- ✓ Create your morning post, whether it is a tip, an inspirational quote, or a link to some interesting content you want to share.

- ✓ Check your Fan Page for activity and reply to comments posted by fans.

- ✓ Update your Page status (check your Topics List for ideas).

Suggested mid-day/evening Facebook activity Schedule (15 min each):

- ✓ Check your Wall for any posts by friends and reply to any you see relevant and interesting.

- ✓ Connect with at least 4-5 people and comment on their posts.

- ✓ Create your mid-day/evening post, whether it is a tip, an inspirational quote, or a link to some interesting content you want to share (different from the morning post).

- ✓ Check your Fan Page for activity and reply to comments posted by fans.
- ✓ Search for pages you may be interested in, and become a fan of at least one.
- ✓ Engage in conversation on two of your favorite pages.
- ✓ Update your Page status (check your Topics List for ideas).

Do not underestimate the power of words and the speed with which information spreads these days. Be mindful of your message, bring value to your community, and you will be successful in creating your PRESENCE, extending your REACH, increasing your VISIBILITY, growing your IMPACT, and in establishing your CREDIBILITY and EXPERTISE.

Make one of your goals this year to learn everything there

is about social media marketing for your business and start implementing what you learn. Along this line, one of my favorite quotes is: "Imperfect action is better than perfect inaction." Get started today!

Other books by Kathryn Rose

Step-by-Step Guides to:

Twitter for Business

SEO/Video Marketing for Business

Linkedin for Business

The Parent's Guide to Facebook

Offers parent's a more in-depth step-by-step guide to privacy, including monitoring your children's online activities and how to protect them on Facebook.

10397053R0

Made in the USA
Lexington, KY
21 July 2011